Kentucky Lullaby

poems by

Matthew Vetter

Finishing Line Press
Georgetown, Kentucky

Kentucky Lullaby

Copyright © 2018 by Matthew Vetter
ISBN 978-1-63534-416-5 First Edition
All rights reserved under International and Pan-American Copyright Conventions. No part of this book may be reproduced in any manner whatsoever without written permission from the publisher, except in the case of brief quotations embodied in critical articles and reviews.

ACKNOWLEDGMENTS

The following poems, or earlier versions of them, first appeared in these publications:

Inscape: "Holler," "Nothing Song" (under the title "Semantics"), "Essay at Eagle Lake"
Journal of Kentucky Studies: "The Shapes of Leaves"
Literary Mama: "Penny Horse," "Counting," "Libation"
Midwest Quarterly: "Lunar Eclipse"
Public Republic: "Hide and Seek,"
Semantikon: "The Box," "Fractures," "Kentucky Night with Child" (under the title "Evening Song"), "Instructions to a Child on a Swing"
Poetry Fix: "To the One-Armed Crawdad Who Pinched My Son"
Red Lion Square: "The River"
American Life in Poetry and *The Louisville Review:* "Wild Flowers"
Zane Traces: "Only Red"

Publisher: Leah Maines
Editor: Christen Kincaid
Cover Art: Art/Map by John Filson, 1784,
Author Photo: Ben Vetter
Cover Design: Elizabeth Maines McCleavy

Printed in the USA on acid-free paper.
Order online: www.finishinglinepress.com
also available on amazon.com

Author inquiries and mail orders:
Finishing Line Press
P. O. Box 1626
Georgetown, Kentucky 40324
U. S. A.

Table of Contents

The River 1

Wild Flowers 2

The Shapes of Leaves 3

In Utero 4

Nothing Song 5

Kentucky Night with Child 6

Lunar Eclipse 7

Counting 8

Fractures 9

The Kiss 10

To the One-Armed Crawdad Who Pinched My Son 11

Holler 13

Hide and Seek 14

He Has Already Made His Country 15

Penny Horse 16

Of Spring and Preschool 18

Instructions to a Child on a Swing 20

Hair Cut 21

The Box 22

Essay at Eagle Lake 23

Elegy for a Beetle, Part III 25

The Tiger Moth 26

Only Red 27

Poem at Sulphur Hollow 28

Libation 29

For my children, for Stacy, for Kentucky

The River

I remember throwing stones,
alone in the gravel lot by the house.

I remember the road,
twisting down to the river,
and that I must have hit a passing car

with one of those stones:

because suddenly a man is in front of me,
at me, asking me where my daddy is,
saying he is going to tell my daddy,
saying he is going to be back.

I remember the dread that filled me,
the dark smudge of it marking me,

like the smell of rubber lingering in the air,
and the black stain of tire on pavement
the man left but never returned to

before my father finished his work,
pulled the belt across my lap
in the brown station wagon,

drove us down that road
and along the Ohio River, home.

How can I tell you that memory haunts me?
That, years later, I am still waiting

for that man to make me pay
for throwing stones, waiting for him to carry
my small body down to the river,

lift his arms up and out and let go.

Wild Flowers

At fifty-six, having left my mother,
my father buys a motorcycle.

I imagine him because
it is the son's sorrowful assignment
to imagine his father:
there, hunched on his mount,
with black boots and jeans

between shifts at the mill,
ripping furrows in the backroads,

past barn and field and silo,
past creek and rock,
past the brown mare, sleek and impertinent,

never slowing until he sees the bull.

He stops, pulls his bike to the side of the road,
where goldenrod and clover grow,

walks up to the fence, admires
its horns, its wet snout snorting and blowing
its breath, its girth, its trampling

of small wild flowers.

The Shapes of Leaves

I want to know the shapes of leaves,
if only to make a place for you among their shadows.

This is one thing we can do:
build sanctuaries on rock formations and creek beds,

wipe away landscapes,
their persistent clutter and debris,

quite simply, make a place to be.

As the Sassafras covers her branches with mittens,
the Sweet Gum showers the earth with green stars,
and the Redbud drops purple blossoms
before it can hang hearts from its limbs.

I would rather lay you down here,
in the shade of these shapes

than on the bathroom floor,
locked against our son's swift knocking on the door.

He has something important to tell us, he shouts,
about the earthworm, about the blackbird,
about the shape of leaves.

I shudder and collapse against you.
The knocking grows more insistent.

In Utero

Lightning pummels
the sky.

It appears obscene
but

perhaps this is what it was like
in the womb,

when your parents made love.
You are frightened

but overjoyed by something
unfamiliar

like a storm.

Together we have transcended something, child.

You are not only a newness,
You bring a death,

an ending to those who have given such hair, eyes, limbs.
Together we bid these children farewell.
Together we grow old.

Nothing Song

My promise to you is this:
I will teach you the names of things

but they will be the names of my choosing.

The moon will be yellow.
The field will be a dark scar,
the river a deep highway.

The rocking chair will be a womb,
the silent winter sky—

a blue smudge on a greater invocation.

I will teach you nothing and nonsense
for nothing but selfish reasons.
This is the nothing song.

But you should know that
your father sings in such ways.
He will hold you close and whisper
all the little names.

He will gather you into arms' fold
and walk out into a clear night

to gaze across the field in the yellow light,
muttering a Kentucky lullaby.

Kentucky Night with Child

It is good to walk in the dark
holding a small child who cries because he wants to be held.

His brother has brought the blade of the scissors
to the manes and tails of the toy horses.
He has scattered the dark hairs across the floor.

I have wanted to turn the mouth of the baby.
I have wanted to turn his wails into orange.

The dark cabinets are like alleyways.

We pass them;
we peer into their currents curiously.

I must do what is possible: clean up this mess of hair,
take walks in the dark hallway,
sing an evening song,

sternly holding him against my narrow body,
colored blue by the light from the window.

In a Kentucky night where the green has gone black,

hear my clear melody,
echoing among the walls and ceiling.

Lunar Eclipse

I like how you throw your cigarette to the grass
and leave me with the wooden rocking chair,

the wetness of your breath lingering
in the frozen air.

I imagine you,
going from room to room, turning off lights,
shutting the cabinets I have left open.

See how stones from the river enter the eyes of our children?
What beautiful stupor sleep ushers.

What will I give them?
The night is theirs.

This shadow passing over the moon makes everything
 explode.

I will not pray tonight.
To pray is to confess solitude, but I am not alone.

To pray in gratitude is to confess coincidence,
to admit to luck or chance,

but everything here I have made,
or helped in the making.

To pray in exaltation is to celebrate that which is not your own.
To pray in petition is to beg.

I will not pray tonight.
I beg for nothing.

I have seen the light between each star brighten
as the red moon goes dark, then bleeds,
then goes dark again.

Counting

The baby sleeps in the afternoon,
small body hunched in on itself like a question mark.

Of course I have to answer it,
walking back to stand above the crib
again and again,

staying long enough to see the small
rise and fall of his back.

When he wakes he will climb
the chair in the kitchen.

His brother will accidentally brush against
that same small part of his back.

He will fall and I will know his pain
because I will count the seconds between

the first scream and the cry that follows,
those breathless, gasping seconds,

every muscle in his body tense:
one, two, three, four, five, six, seven, eight, nine, ten.

It's winter now.
It's years later I think.

And I remember it all through my own words.
I won't talk. I can't speak of this.

Fractures

Prying open a bottle of beer,
I think of my son: only one year old.

But if the skull could talk,
it would confess a dozen knocks and falls—

a table's corner,
the wet tile of the bathroom
after I so carefully washed his feet, hands, genitals;

the smack of the screen door;
the porch swing,
its red wagon and hanging baskets of petunias.

What violence is this? Is this what it takes?
Is this the way it is?

The accidents are senseless.
The children are senseless.

They tape green maple leaves to the walls
and rip the flowers from their vase,

then offer them to us like some kind of gift.

Their mother and I pace the house all night,
sullen and refusing to speak to each other.

What were the reasons? Can we remember them?
Do we want to?

The Kiss

Have you ever been kissed by a one-year old boy,
woken by his wet mouth grazing your own?

It is intentional—yes, but how clumsy, how coy:
his soft, moist lips, so tender, so unknown

meeting the slight reluctance of my mouth, maybe
only plaque or halitosis, but maybe something worse.

It's enough to make me stop and shout, "Baby,
don't put your mouth on that," as often I've rehearsed

"Don't put that in your mouth!" when he tries
(just a taste) the dog food, the ink pen, a small stone

from the driveway. I turn his face to mine to pry
apart the jaws. The tooth bites the finger: bone to bone.

Perhaps I should be thankful he is so free with them.
Still, I can't stop thinking of the places our lips have been.

To the One-Armed Crawdad Who Pinched My Son

I call it an arm,
when it was nothing so human,

really a claw,
a pincher you flung straight out
to make your body long,

to glide slowly backwards, lobster-like,
in a dream of cold spring creek water.

I could tell your sluggishness
and prodded you up against a mound of dirt and rock.

To the delight of my son I held you between two fingers,
right behind your one and only pincher,
which you twisted and snapped open and shut
before laying you back down in the mud of the creek-bed.

Who took your claw, crawdad?
What broke you against the rock or log?

What do you know of my son who grabs at you now,
palm and fist, in imitation of his daddy
and ignorant of the delicacy needed;
what can you do but pinch?

Crawdad, I question your ignorance before I can know
ignorance is at the heart of a threat like this.
All danger comes from unknowing,
but not all danger comes from innocence.

I can't eat you, crawdad,
you're too small and muddy.
I can't mend you;
so stupidly I tend to my own
who shrieks with the quick prick of your pinch.

I swing his small body up to rest against my hips.
I kiss his finger as the smell of excrement rises
from the diaper beneath his clothing.

Its stench holds us together.
It surrounds us in our own human promises.

Holler

Not the holler of a tiger caught by the toe
Not the eeny, meeny, miny, moe.

Not the holler you give me when I'm still laid up in bed
with the boys' breakfasts uneaten,

and both of them tearing through the house
like the mad bulls of Pamplona.

Not the holler, not even the hollow
of a small valley between two hills
with a little creek that runs through it

and four red-winged blackbirds flying into the wind, unable
to get anywhere for a moment, before perching
on the branch of a maple.

No.

This holler, your holler,
with the weight of my body crushing into you,
with the boys asleep in their beds and a line of toy fire trucks
turning the blue carpet of the playroom red.

Not a bellow or complaint
but something between a scream and a breath
like the sound of one bright bell,

then another, and another,
then hundreds of bells,

so that it is impossible to hear them separately
and impossible to know the reason they were rung.

Hide and Seek

It is easy to find you, child,
because you want to be found.

You hide in the same place every time:
crouching in a pile of your mother's shoes,
beneath a canopy of her dresses.

You knock on the folding closet doors
if it takes me too long,
impatient for the thrill of discovery.

Now it is my turn.

Count to ten,
I tell you as I walk to the bathroom.

I step into the tub and pull the curtain,
the only witness the whiskers in the sink.

Unlike you, I am playing to hide.

Each time you pass me over,
mistakenly looking in all the wrong places,
only encourages me to be quieter,

to let my breathing slow and soften.

I have felt this before,
I want to disappear, but it is not a
sullen or dark feeling- it is just

that I cannot go deep enough
into the quiet places of my body.

He Has Already Made His Country

The map the child draws
becomes a linking of line and paper, of mirror and space.

In the pastiche beyond,
across the newness of imaginary states,
everything is play for this one.

Everything is play for every child:
pacific, isthmus, coast. The smell of a shape,
the shape of a boy who draws a map,

who sees for the first time,
how bodies meet, how things connect
like puzzles in the aboriginal beginning.

Dear little boy. Don't follow your map away from me.

But he has already made his country.
Drawing boundaries and naming spaces,
he has already made his country. It is not Kentucky.

Why do we piece things together?
How does the father learn to play like that?
He must stand on the shadow-line, on the equator,
always seeing two likenesses.

This is how we create our worlds.
The lines and words make it so.

Too soon we diverge,
too soon construct dissimilar conceptions of earth.
Linger, child, linger with me in this place.

Penny Horse

It's not for apples, though
that is not a bad idea.

And I haven't been sent for milk or eggs or flour.
In fact, I am list-less,

but accompanied by my four-year-old son
who perches on the lip of the cart,
which he insists is not a cart,
but a train, a boat, a motorcycle.

I throw a few items into its saddlebag,
so as not to seem suspicious:

so that we are not empty-handed
as we approach the check-out lanes.

No, I do not need any help,
and we are in the lobby
and in the corner is the reason for the trip:

I hand him a penny and lift him up,
watch as he straddles it,
drops the coin into the slot.

Watch as he urges the animal forward and faster,
digs his bony heels into its sides,

watch and they are through the sliding glass doors,
crossing the parking lot,

and I am left alone,
desperately clutching my bags,

nodding my head and humming along
to the song of a horseless carousel
playing Rossini's Overture to *William Tell*.

Of Spring and Preschool

Almost always first the pear tree,
smelling like a stray dog,

all white
and bobbing in a sea of new green.

Then daffodils, what you call Easter flowers,
clusters of tiger lily reeds,

and the strange, familiar smell of warm, growing things.
Like cow manure,

the effluvia of straw and wild onions
on the first day of sun,

real sun that melts like butter on your face.

And days of rain too, with wind scattering the water
across your neck almost like

the salt spray of the ocean
and the tiny hairs sticking up there, ah,
just long enough for you to remember:

the morning walk down the long hallway,
slouched a bit to hold your son's hand.
Rows and rows of artwork covering the walls,

the tiny handprints
on colored construction paper.

In the classroom,
miniature tables and chairs,
the teacher turns and bends among the children,
tucking a length of hair behind her ear

as voices begin to swell and rise and sing:
Good morning, good morning, good morning to you.
The day is beginning, there's so much to do.

Instructions to a Child on a Swing

On your way up,
lean back and stretch your legs up and out.

On your way back,
push your body forward and tuck your legs in.

It's not an oracle, this, or even a candle,
more like a Sisyphean pendulum.

It swings us all forward
for a moment, making us believe

we were meant
to be among molecules like this:

sun, bird, cloud.
Too soon, we are falling again,

into the heaviness
of earth and excrement,

into corporeality,
the truth of blood and semen
and the bodies we never asked for.

Hair Cut

Always I want to remember us this way:

your blade poised above my head,
me in a chair you've taken from the kitchen
and dragged into the back yard.

Silence, now, enough to hear
the snip, snip, snip of your scissors.

In your hands, wife, I am a string-less marionette.
You push my head this way and that.

We can't stop disorder,
only a temporary staving is truly possible.

It is enough; cut it clean and simple,
something like our alliance, our quotidian vengeance.

Longer on top, please, and trim around the ears.
This is the way I want to remember us always.

My dull brown hair falls from your blade.
My dull brown hair looks good against the tall green grass.

Our son is next, with talk of nests.
He is sure the birds will put our hair to good use.
Nothing is wasted.

Something intricate and soft.
Something to give the tree another purpose.

The Box

It is a clear plastic box, with a grated top to let the air in.
The child traps a moth but cannot leave it alone.

He drops a stone, a clod of dirt, a single blade of grass.
He gives the whole thing a shake, tosses it back and forth

between tiny pink hands. He takes it by the wings, dusty and dry
between his fingers. He peers into its dull and black eyes.

The moth does not look back and I cannot look at either of them.
He has kept us as well: mother and father, to look

closely into our eyes, to implore, to examine, to ask.
We don't want to escape. To escape would be to surrender.

But we're so tired, nonetheless. Exhausted, we sit in front
of windows as the sky darkens and fireflies begin to dance

under the maples. I search the house. He will want a jar.
He will want holes punched in the lid. He will want forceps.

Essay at Eagle Lake

Twice the doe has strayed to the bottom of the hollow,

where chicory and goldenrod grow,
where tree line meets path,
and path meets water.

And twice have I met her, and once looked for her.

I have found geese as well.
I run at them just to see their excited departure.
I want to watch them fly away from my simple violence.

Of course I stumble and fall.
I'm still young.

Without my sons, I'm afraid I am as my father:
impatient for the infinite.

I hunger.

I look for the doe and I look at her long.
I feed on her soft doe-eyes.

I brush the gnat from my eye.
as she twitches her ear,
and stamps her hind leg to shake off the horsefly.

I never stop looking.
I cannot let go of the strange, bestial embrace of our gaze.
I fill myself like a tick until I am

satisfied as if

my blood-gorged body hung
from the white fur of her belly.

We are in this world together for a moment
and then she is gone,
bounding away like she was made for this dream.

I must return, too.
Of course I recite these lines to myself along the way.
I do not want to forget them.

These things are valuable to me:
the doe, the geese, the purple and yellow
of the chicory and the goldenrod.

It is because I can use them again and again
that I emerge from the woods
like a madman, a gadabout, a poetaster,

dirt-drenched and sweating, mumbling, always
mumbling to myself.

Elegy for a Beetle, Part III

For the tiny grave lasts but one day,
and in the morning my son,

together now with his younger brother,
digs up the coffin and exhumes the body.

The youngest boy rips the beetle into three parts,
and the older one, who was so caring,
who was so intent on a proper

and beautiful funeral
is not even bothered.

How easily he dismisses all of my sentiment and meaning.
How I praised him for his thoughtful insect burial.

How easily he leaves me
with nothing to celebrate or understand.

I cannot choose between empathy and destruction
because I cannot know which was sincere.

Only that in the aporia between the two,
there is little but unknowing,

the plundering of tombs for insignificant trinkets,

and always,
only senselessness.

The Tiger Moth

Because the baby smiles in the ecstasy of a dream,
because I have read three stories to our son,
because the frogs chirp in the pond

and the maples anticipate
the moment of clarity that comes
with the flash of a firefly,

because it is summer,
I love you.

But it could have been anything:
a red-winged blackbird among the lilac,

the quiet way a fire breathes, and is given breath,
the shadow of a tiger moth against a screen,
wanting only one thing:

to be closer, and closer, and closer
to the warmth, the strength, the beauty of the light.

Only Red

I wanted to write about its ferocity,
about how devastating it was,
how violent, how heartbreaking,

how terrible, destructive, beautiful.
How it took the light from the window
in just a certain way, how it made me feel,

how it reminded me of something
I had long forgotten, and how it might
make others remember something too,

how wherever I went, whatever else there was
just melted away. It had this power.
How I could look in the rearview mirror

on the street I drive every day and how
I could see it and just that glance
could take my breath away,

could make me renounce everything.

But it was only hair. My son's red hair,
shaggy, needing a trim, the sweat
from his brow making it cling to his face.

How could I write about that?
Who would want to read it?

Poem at Sulphur Hollow

I don't need to tell you
I have claimed the biggest, moss-covered rock,
to sit with my son and watch dart from tree to tree
the black and yellow bird who brought me here.

What does she know, I wonder, of the back half of the Ford
I found buried in the hillside, the lock of its trunk
still shining among the rust and decay.

All around us, mast from oaks and maples waits
to be scavenged, stored, peeled.

The skin of the oak nut is scored,
divided like the fruit of an orange
into so many sections.

My son wants to gather as many as he can,

wants to throw them down the hollow,
wants to add one small sound to the winter roar of wind

blowing against a thousand dead dry leaves all at once.

Now there's a low wailing across the fields,
beyond the tree line that borders the edge of Sulphur Hollow.

I stand and turn my head.
I want to know the animal that would cry like that.

Libation

Who will I thank for this?
The dandelions have gone to seed.

My son has brought the tallest stalk,
and tiptoed over carefully
to protect its perfect globe,

a clock of white parachutes.

We take turns blowing but
my son is so hungry.

He says he wants to eat the world.

The biggest thing
is the whole world, he says.

I am so thirsty I could drink the world.

He stuffs goldenrod into an empty coke bottle
and offers it up to me.

Of this I drink heartily and with no regrets.
There is another brimming with crisp, dead, dry leaves.

Assistant Professor of English at Indiana University of Pennsylvania, **Matthew Vetter** earned his Ph.D. from Ohio University. He also holds an M.A. in English Literature from Morehead State University and an M.F.A. in Poetry from Spalding University. His poems have appeared in numerous national and regional literary journals including *Midwest Quarterly, American Life in Poetry, The Louisville Review,* and *The Journal of Kentucky Studies.* A Pushcart Prize and AWP Intro Award nominee, Vetter was the 2009 winner of the Danny Miller Memorial Award. He lives in Indiana, Pennsylvania with his wife Stacy and three children.

www.ingramcontent.com/pod-product-compliance
Lightning Source LLC
LaVergne TN
LVHW041507070426
835507LV00012B/1387